Latin Elements - Part One

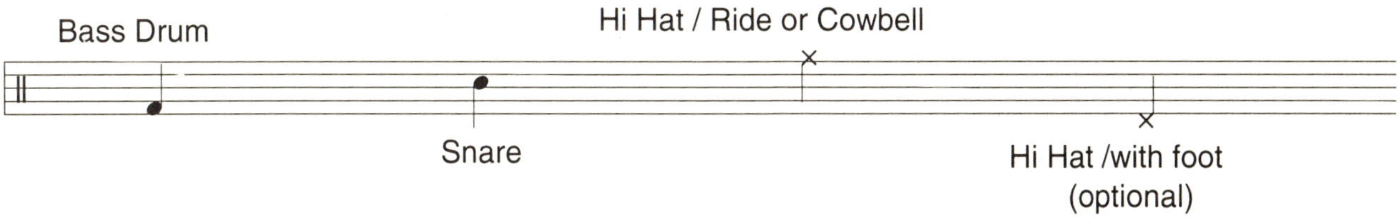

In this tutorial we will focus on keeping steady 16th notes between the hi hat and snare while playing a samba ostinato on the bass drum.
All unaccented snare drum notes should be played very light or ghosted.
On the CD I accent the "and" of the beat on the hi hat.

Web Sites
www.frankbriggs.com
www.melbay.com

Latin Elements - Part One

1

2

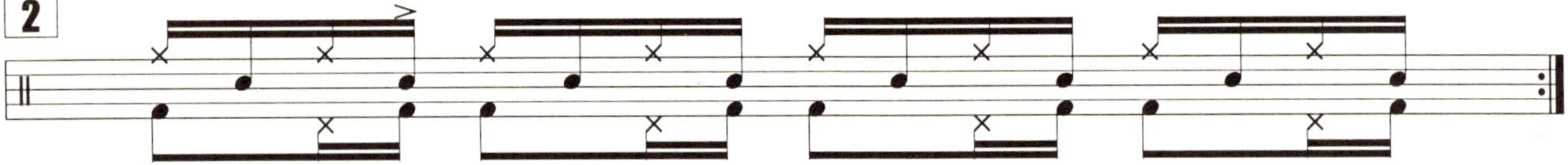

3

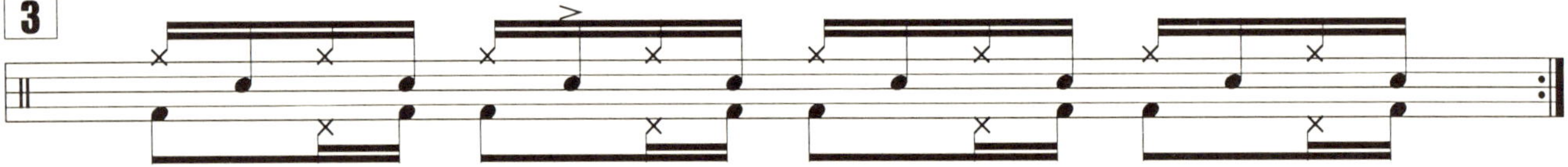

Mel Bay's

LATIN ELEMENTS

FOR THE DRUM SET

By Frank Briggs

MEL BAY

QWIKGUIDE®

Visit us on the Web at http://www.melbay.com – E-mail us at email@melbay.com

Part One

Part Two

Latin Elements - Part One

4

5

6

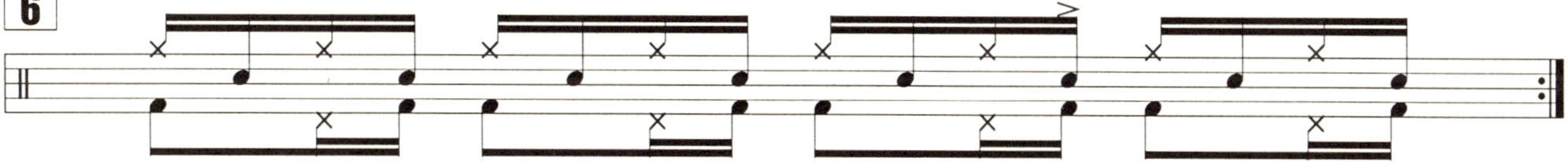

Latin Elements - Part One

7

8

9

Latin Elements - Part One

10

11

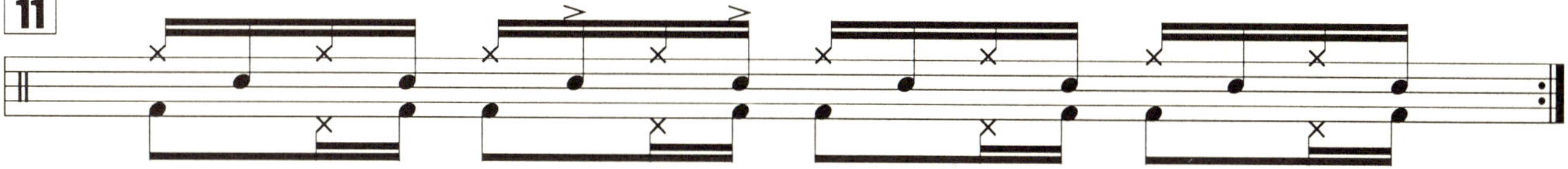

12

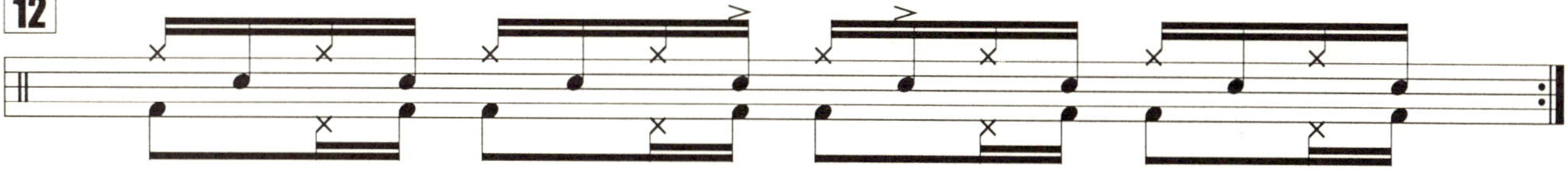

Latin Elements - Part One

13

14

15

Latin Elements - Part One

16

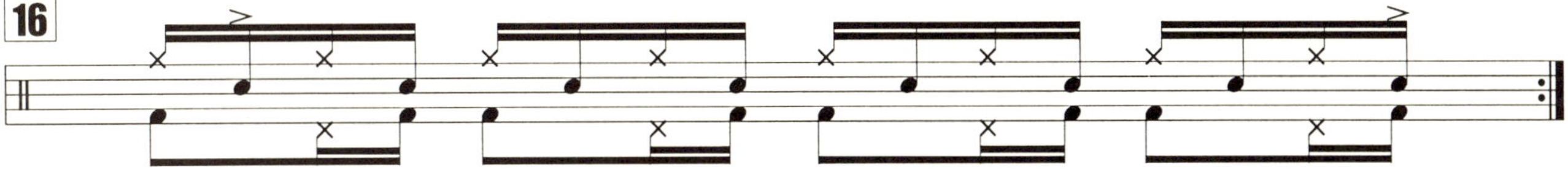

17

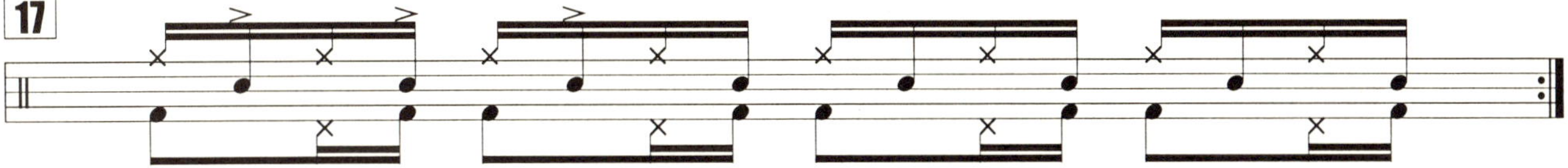

18

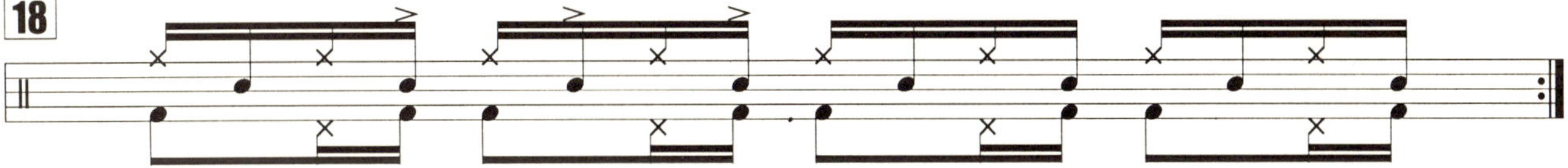

Latin Elements - Part One

19

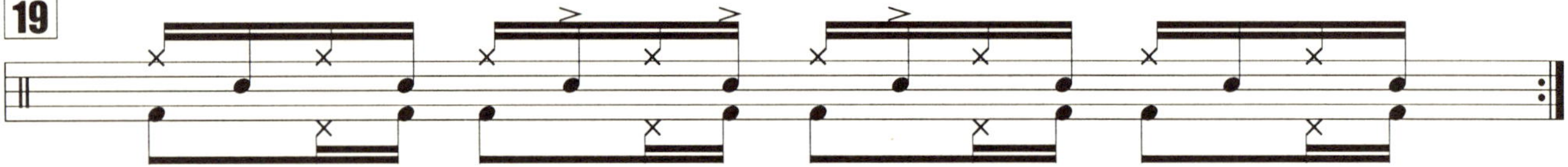

20

21

Latin Elements - Part One

22

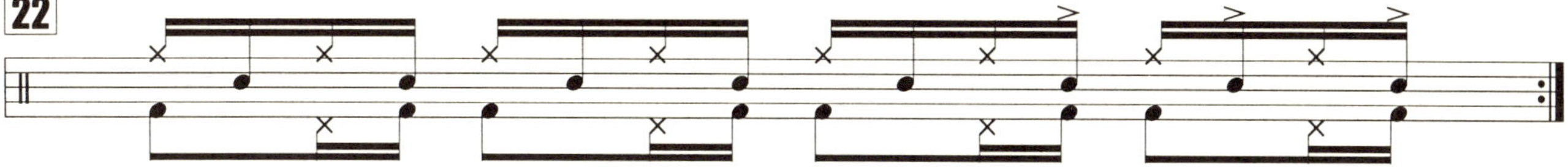

23

24

Latin Elements - Part One

25

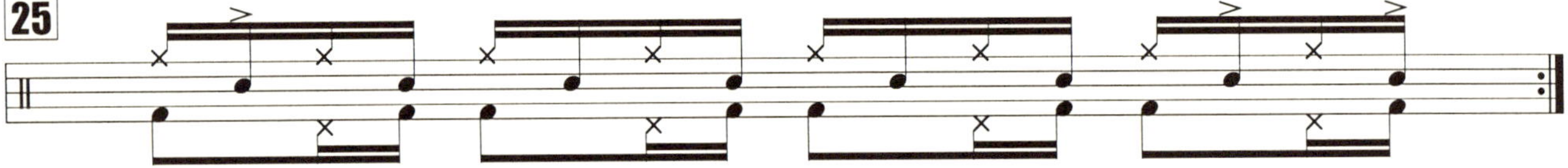

26

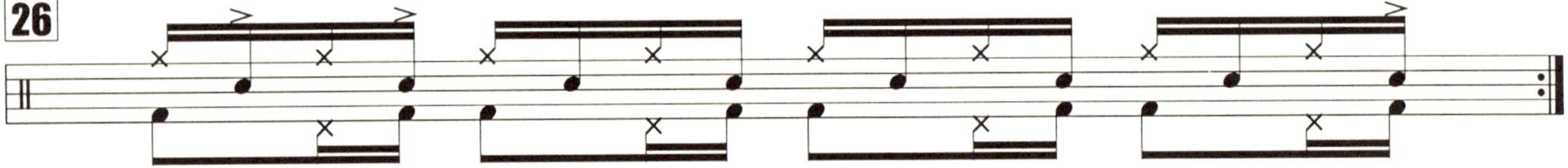

27

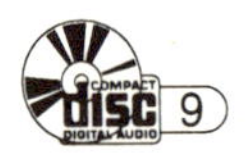

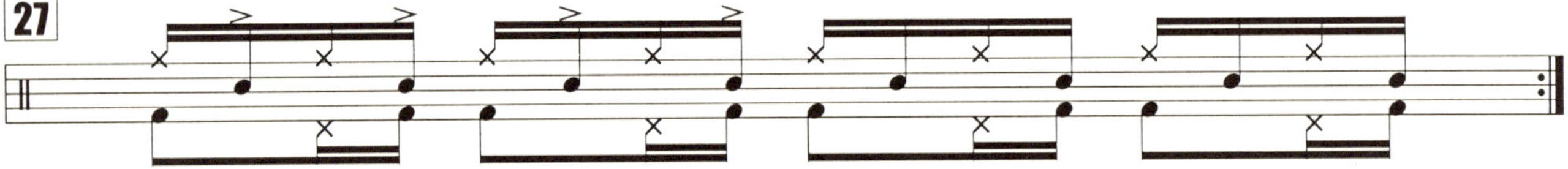

Latin Elements - Part One

28

29

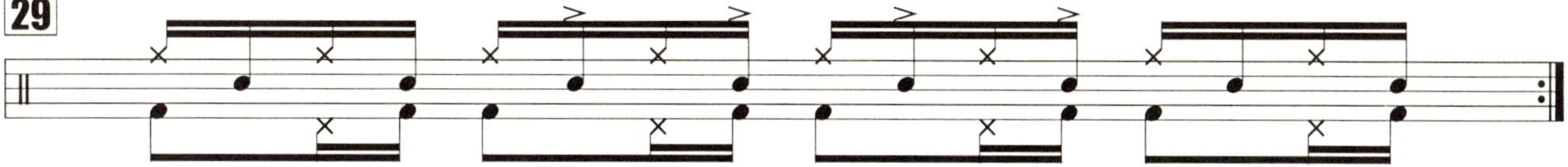

30

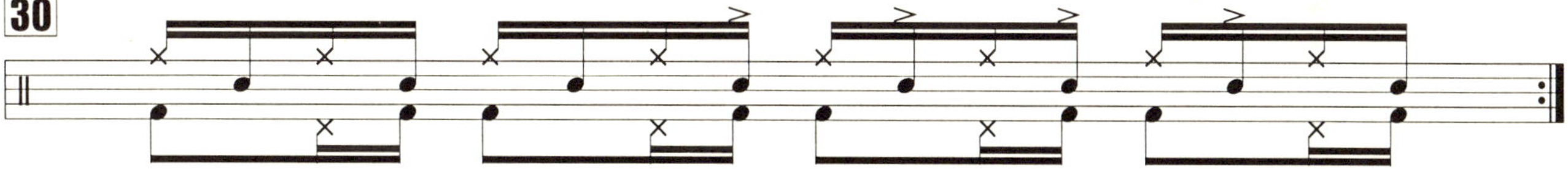

Latin Elements - Part One

31

32

33

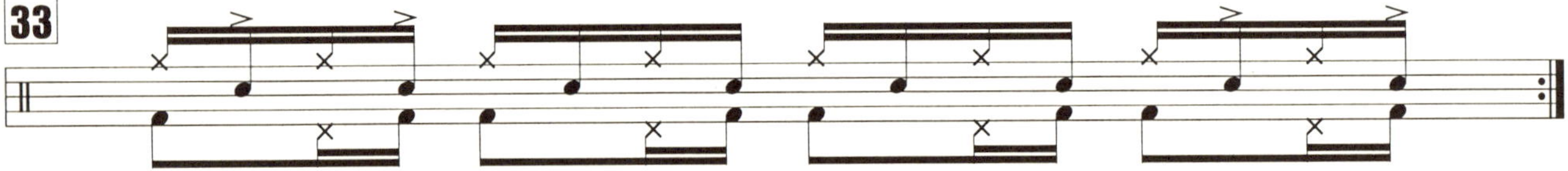

Latin Elements - Part One

34

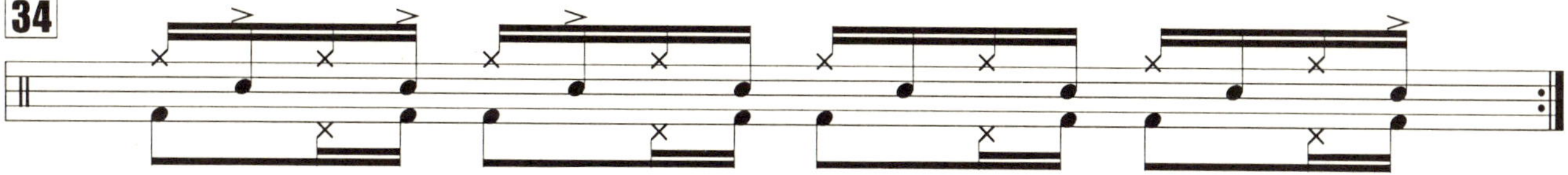

35

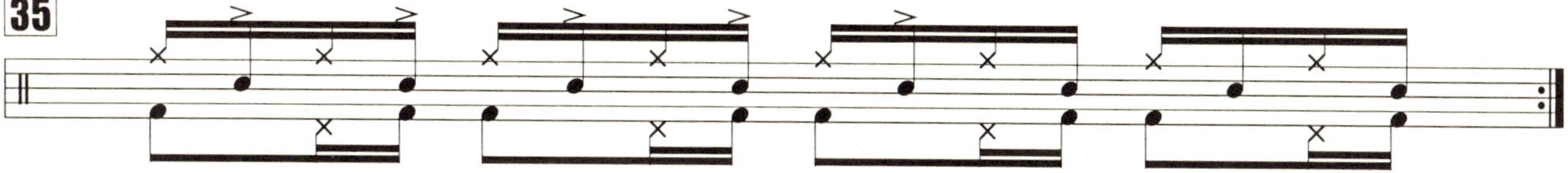

36

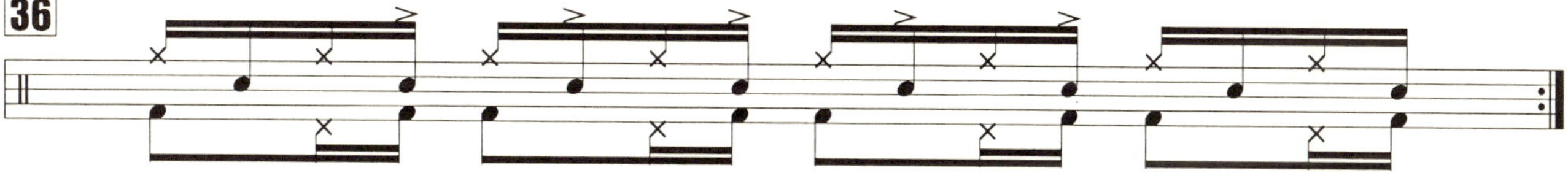

Latin Elements - Part One

37

38

39

COMPACT DISC DIGITAL AUDIO 14

Latin Elements - Part One

40

41

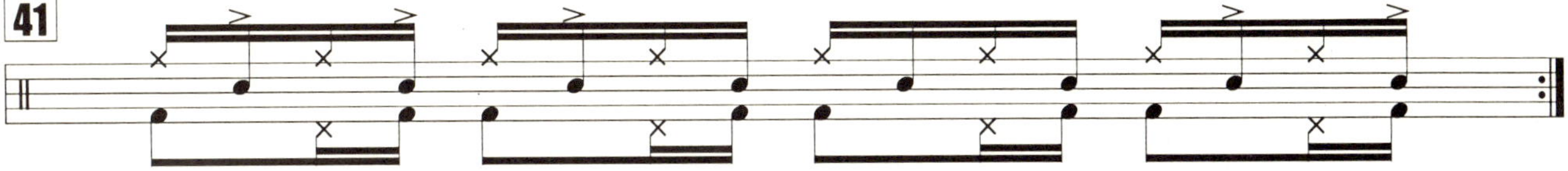

42

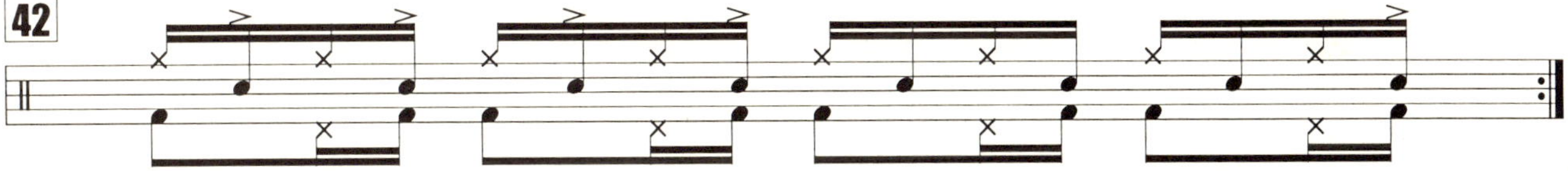

Latin Elements - Part One

43

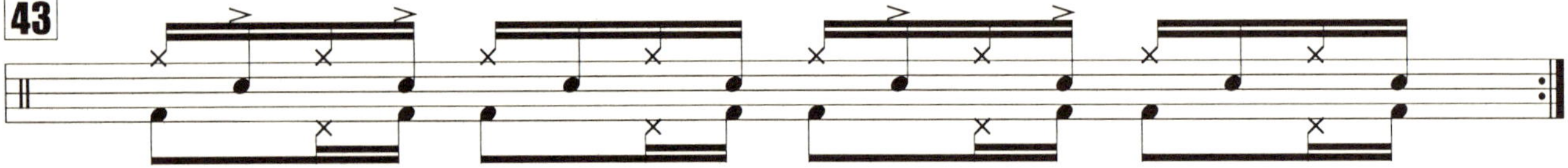

44

45

Latin Elements - Part One

46

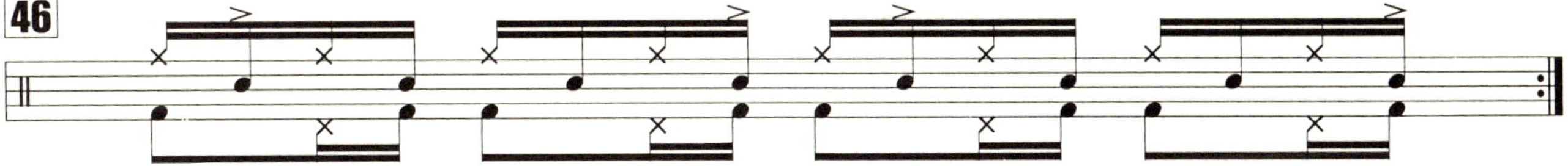

47

48

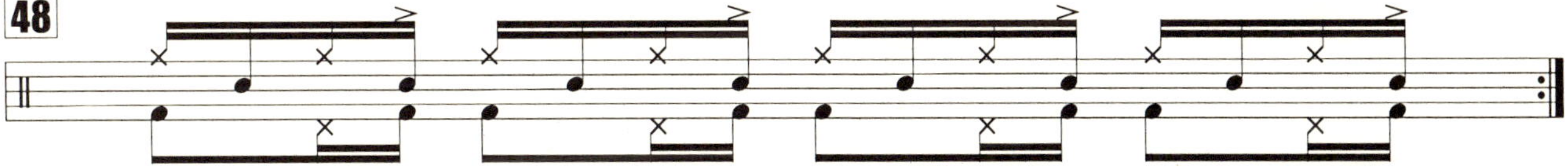

17

Latin Elements - Part One

49

50

51

Latin Elements - Part One

52

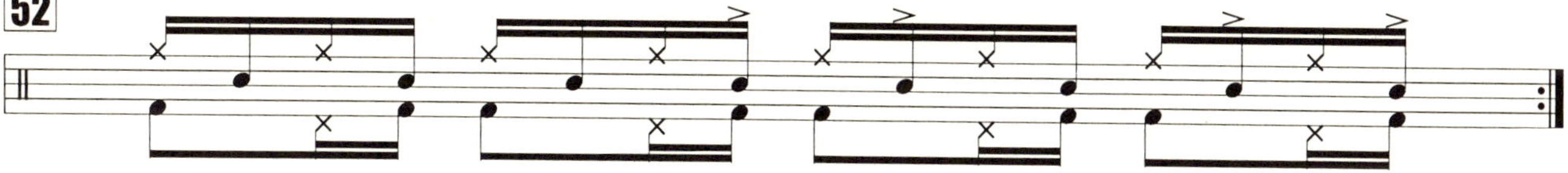

53

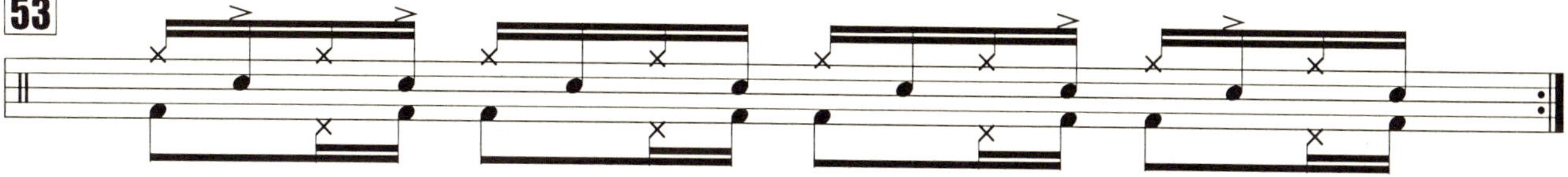

54

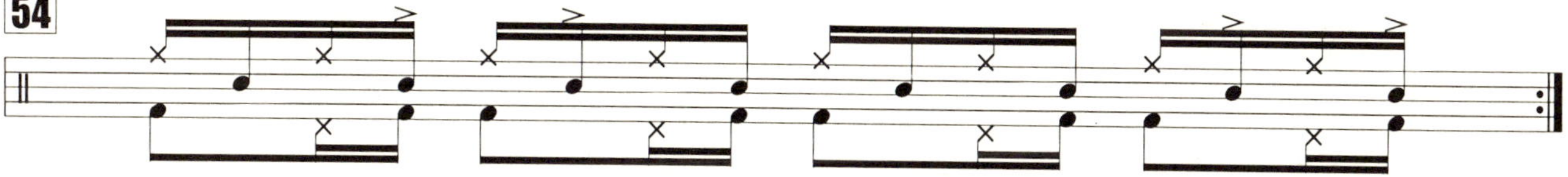

Latin Elements - Part One

55

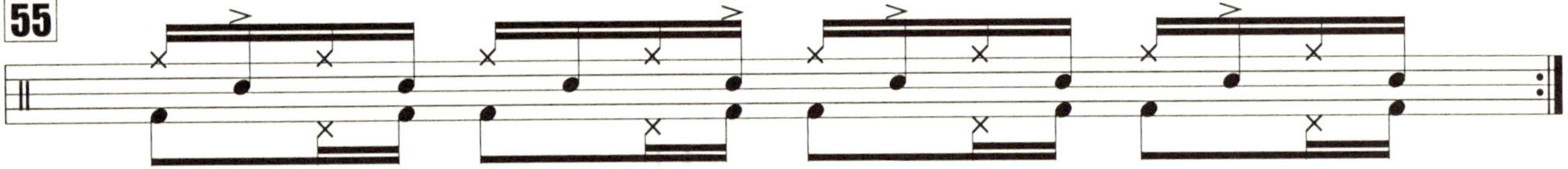

56

57

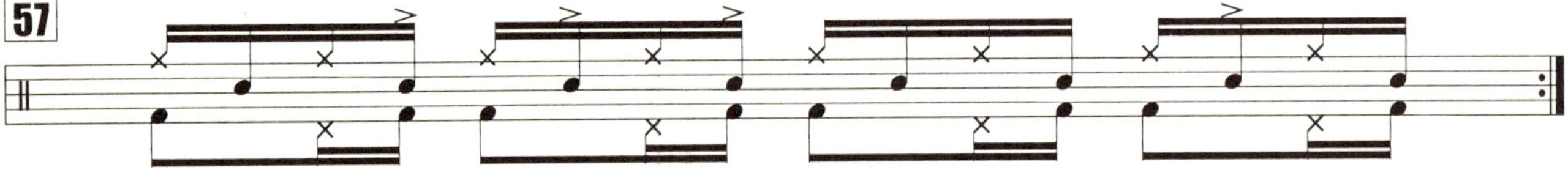

20

Latin Elements - Part One

58

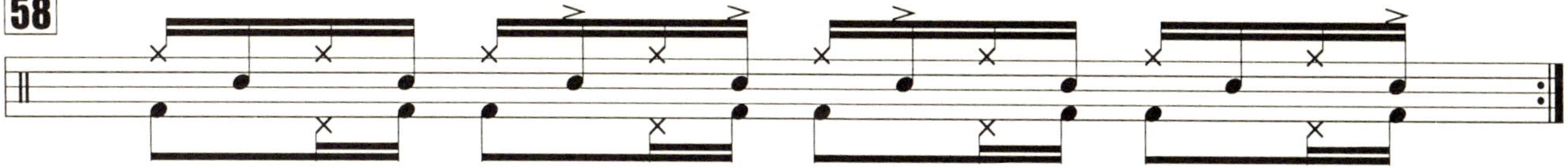

59

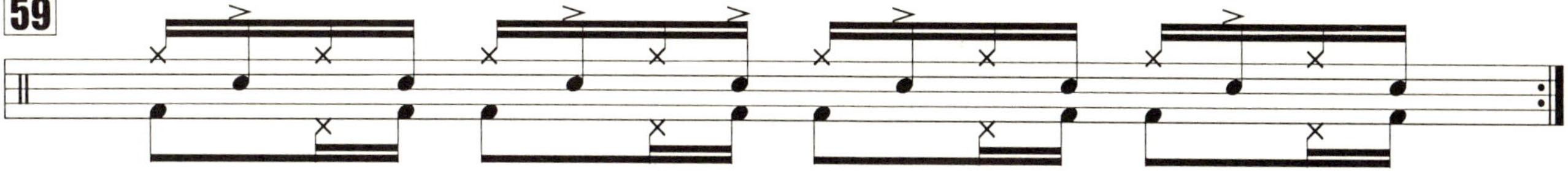

60

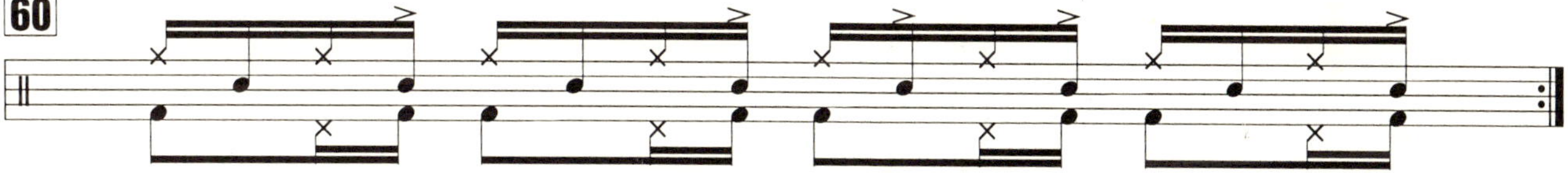

Latin Elements - Part One

61

62

63

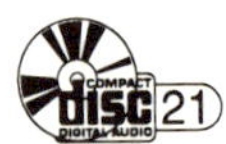

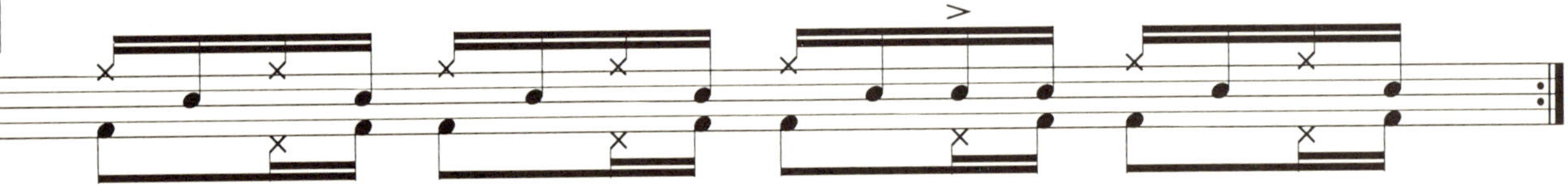

Note* All unaccented notes should be played lightly or "ghosted"

Right Hand Accents

Latin Elements - Part One

64

65

66

Latin Elements - Part One

67

68

69

Latin Elements - Part One

70

71

72

Latin Elements - Part One

73

74

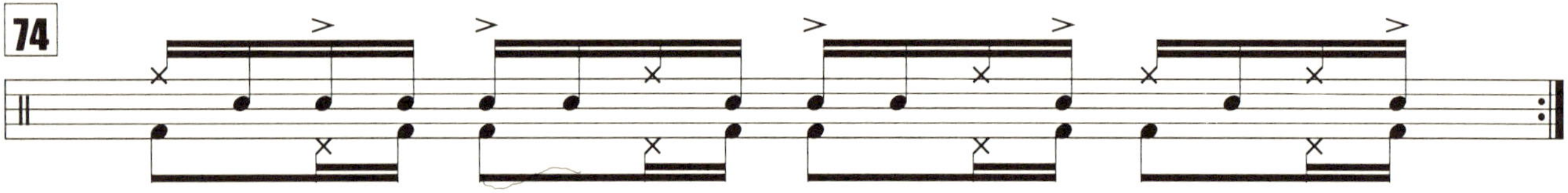

75

Latin Elements - Part One

76

77

78

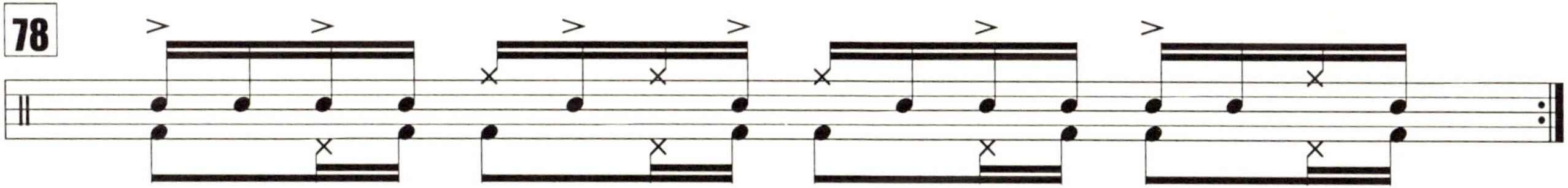

Latin Elements - Part One

79

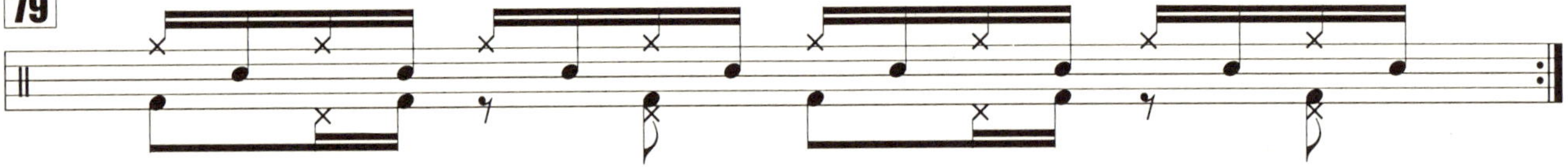

80

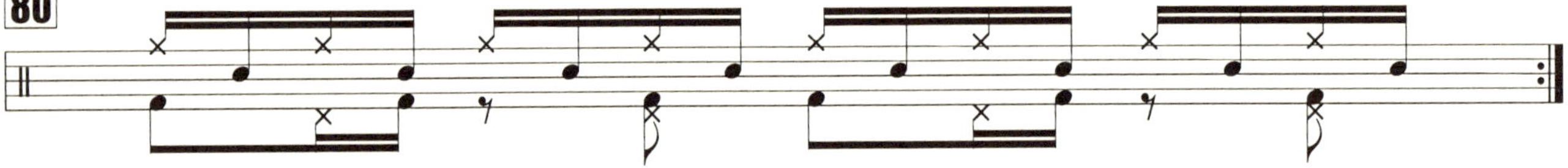

81

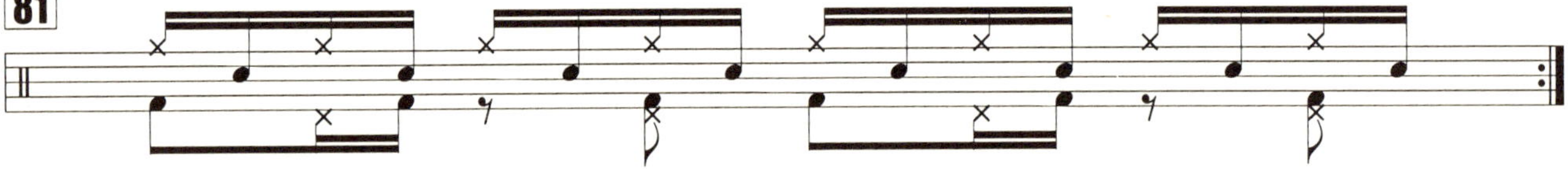

Use the following three pages as templates to write your own accents

Latin Elements - Part One

82

83

84

Latin Elements - Part One

85

86

87

This page has been left blank intentionally

Latin Elements - Part Two

In this tutorial we will focus on keeping steady 16th notes between the hi hat and snare while playing an ostinato on the bass drum.
All unaccented snare drum notes should be played very light or ghosted.
On the CD I accent the ands on the hi hat with my right hand.
The left foot can be added when the right hand part is moved to the ride cymbal
Experiment... you can also use these as "Second Line" patterns by swinging the feel.

Web Sites
www.frankbriggs.com
www.melbay.com

Latin Elements - Part Two

1

2

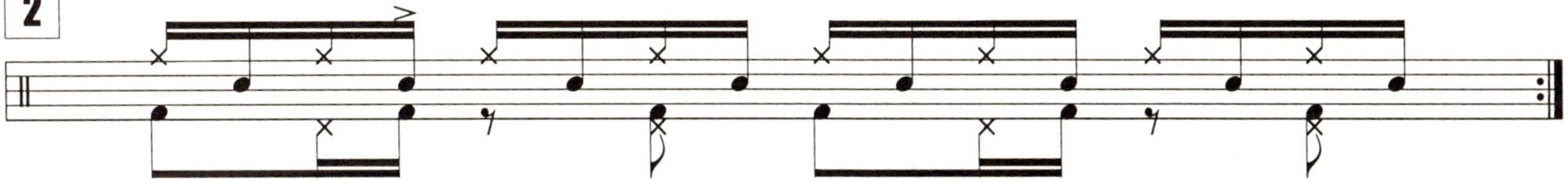

3

Latin Elements - Part Two

4

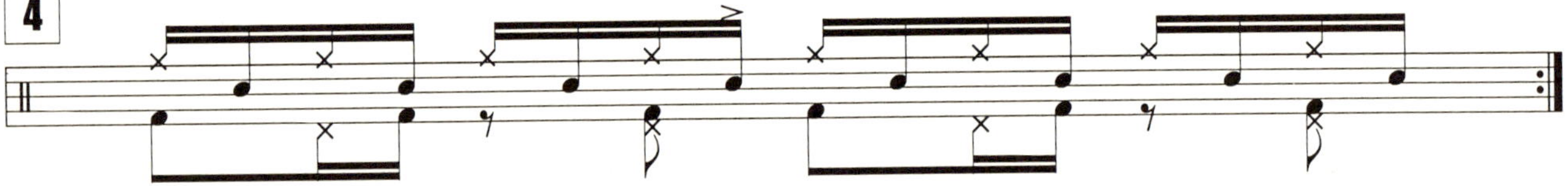

5

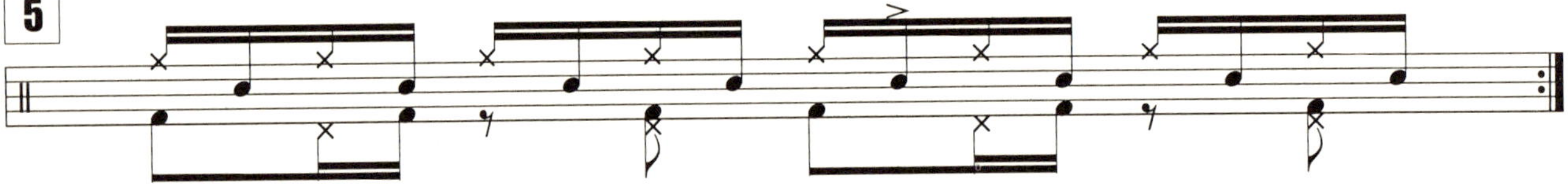

6

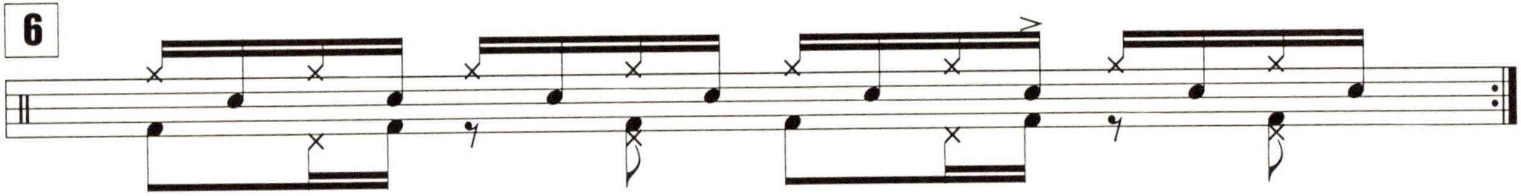

Latin Elements - Part Two

7

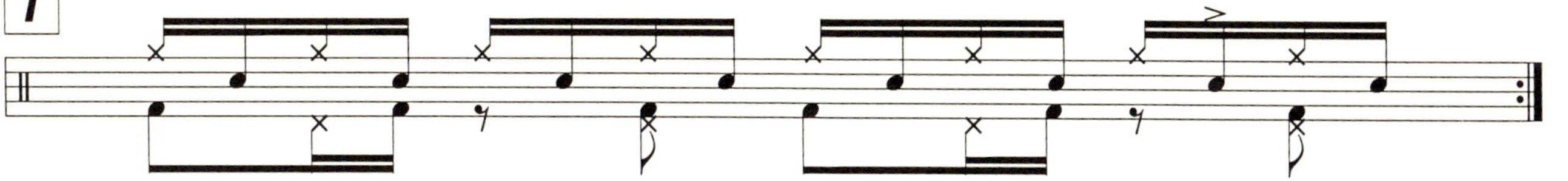

8

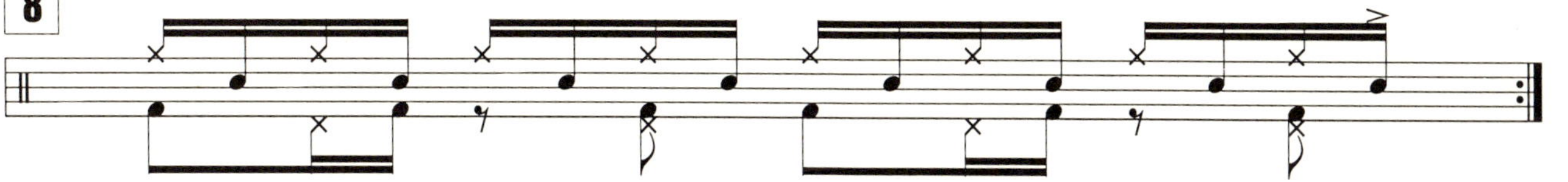

9

Latin Elements - Part Two

10

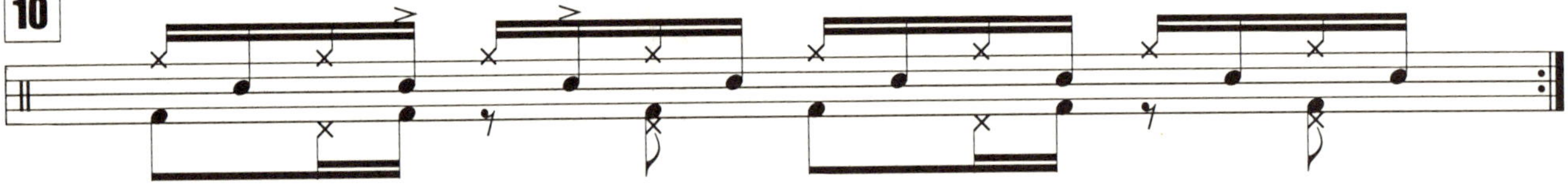

11

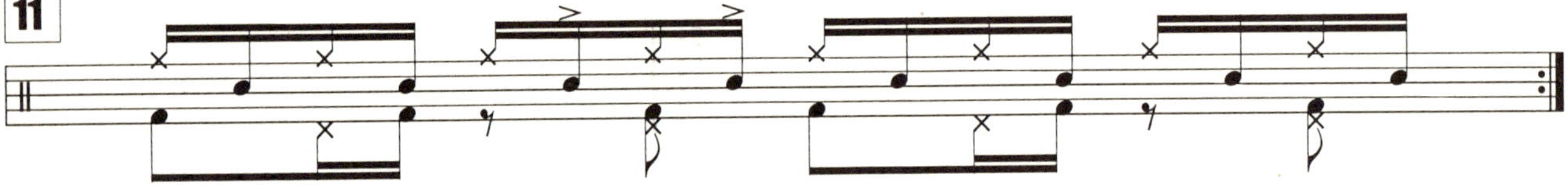

12

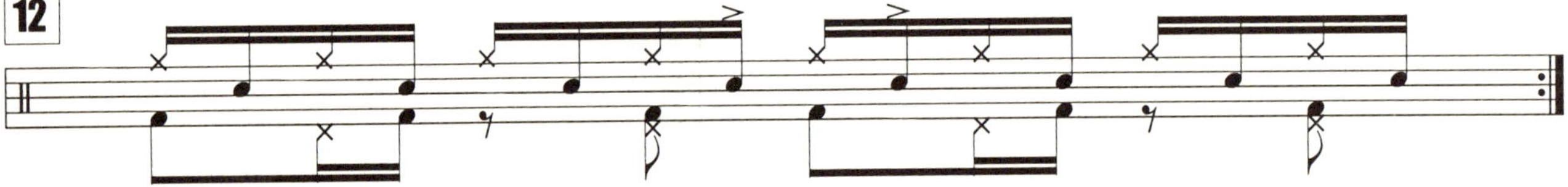

COMPACT disc DIGITAL AUDIO 31

Latin Elements - Part Two

13

14

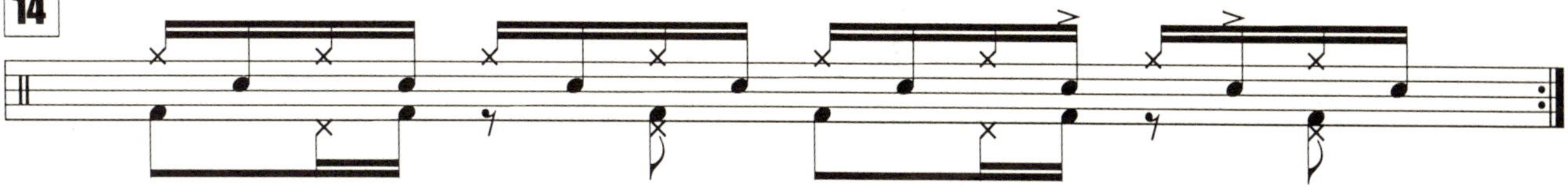

15

Latin Elements - Part Two

16

17

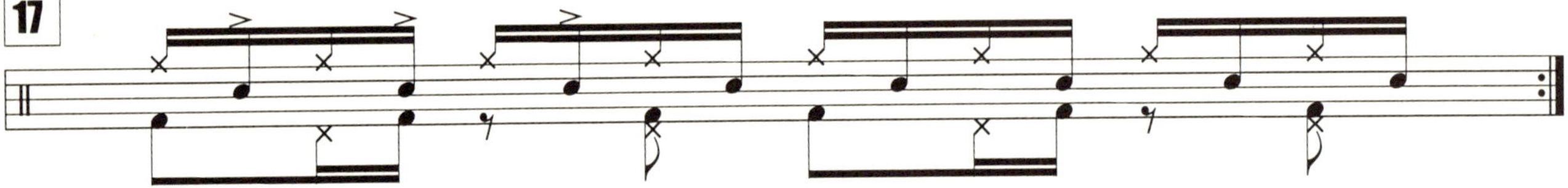

18

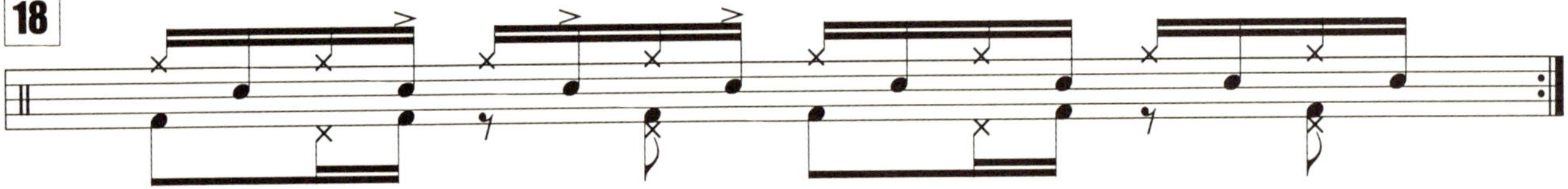

33

Latin Elements - Part Two

19

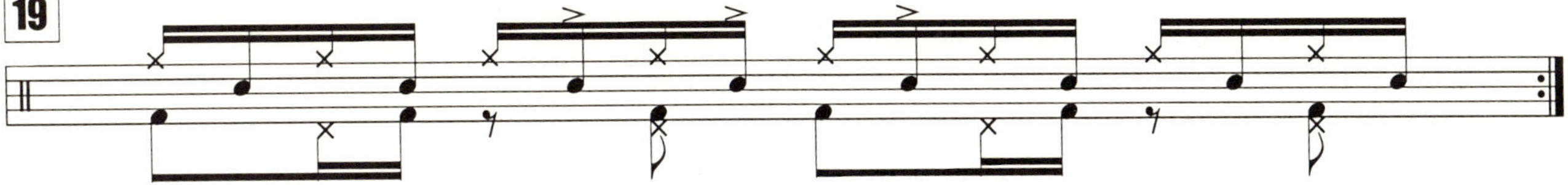

20

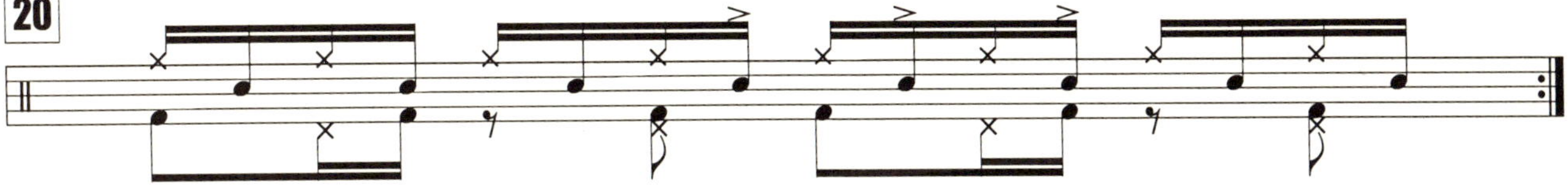

21

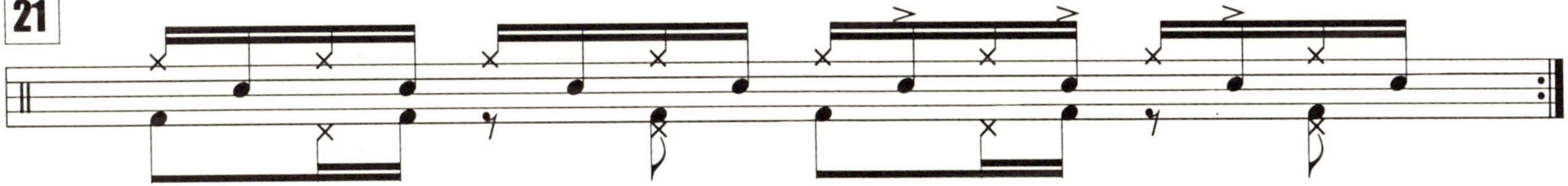

Latin Elements - Part Two

22

23

24

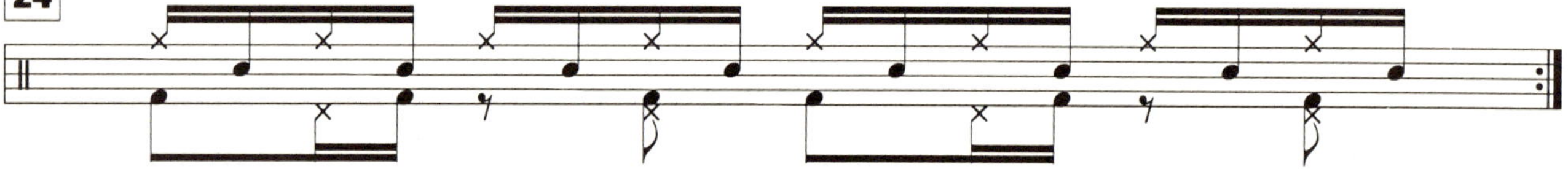

Latin Elements - Part Two

25

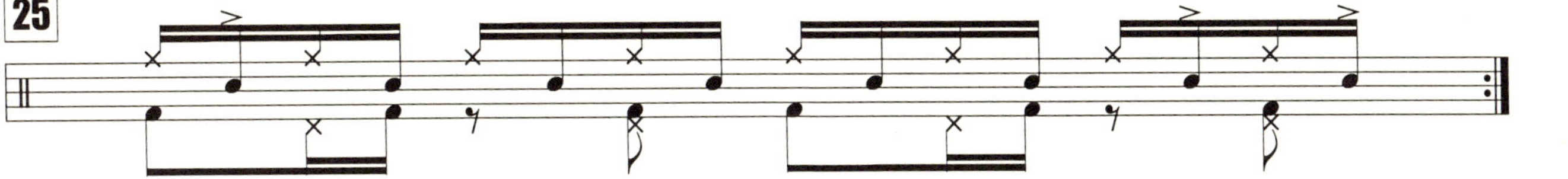

26

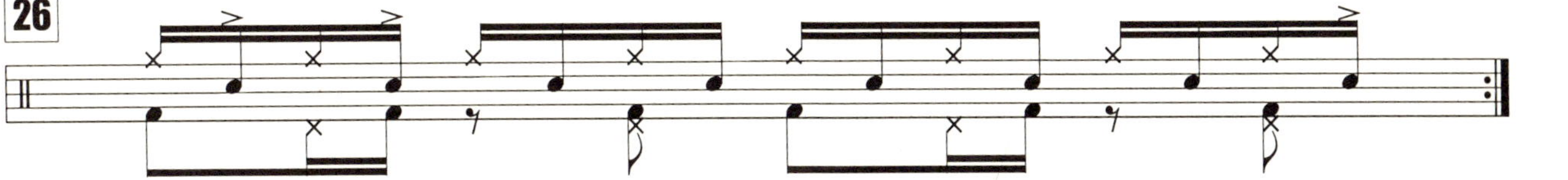

27

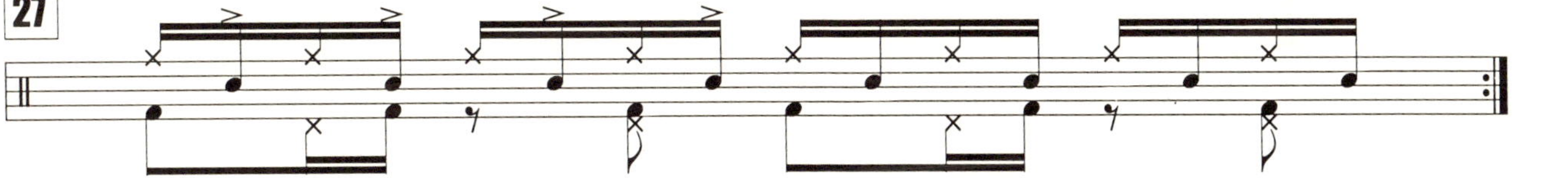

Latin Elements - Part Two

28

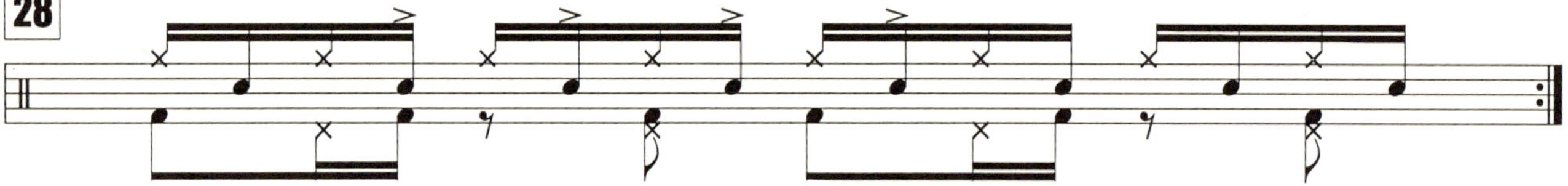

29

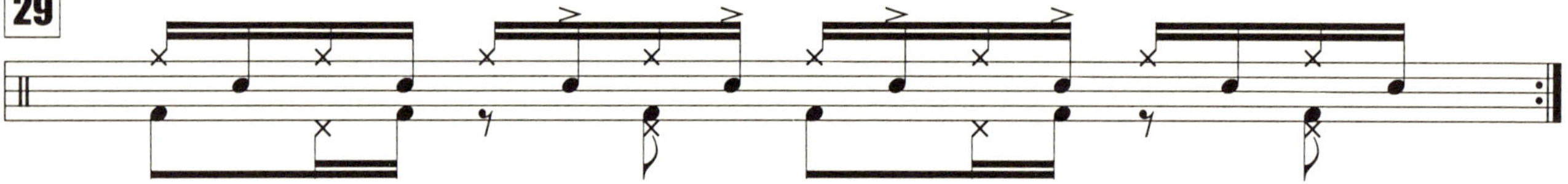

30

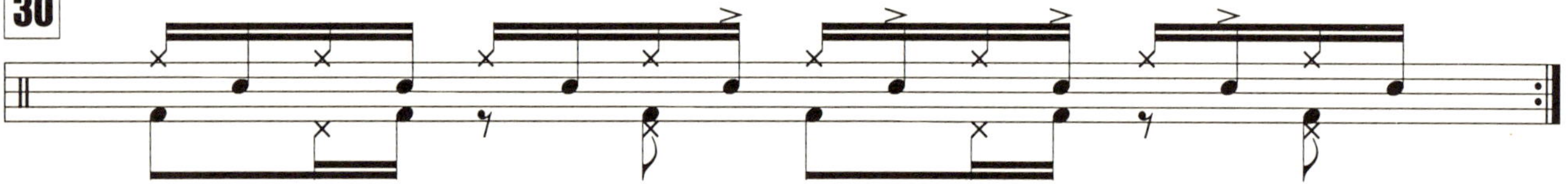

Latin Elements - Part Two

31

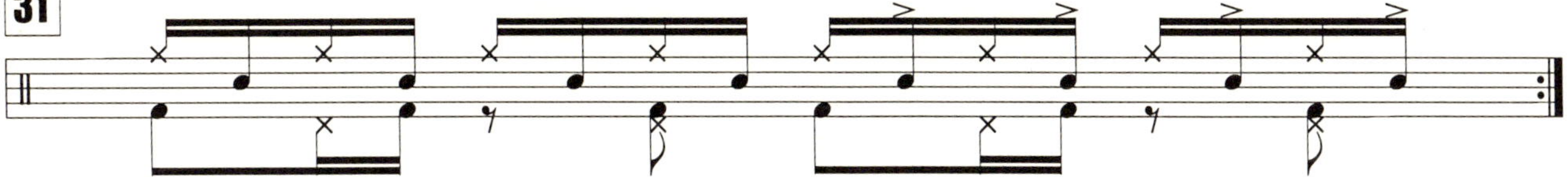

32

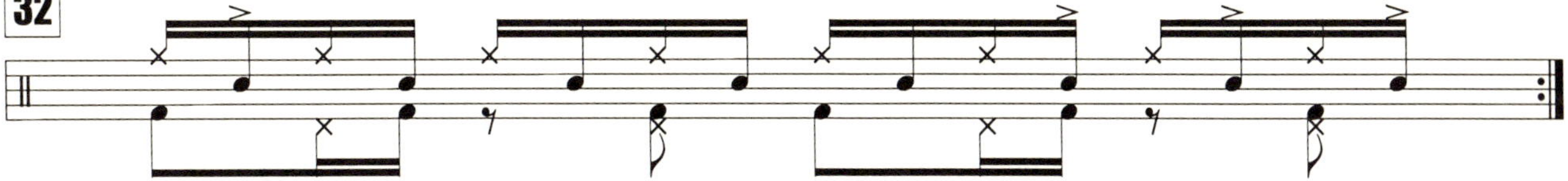

33

Latin Elements - Part Two

34

35

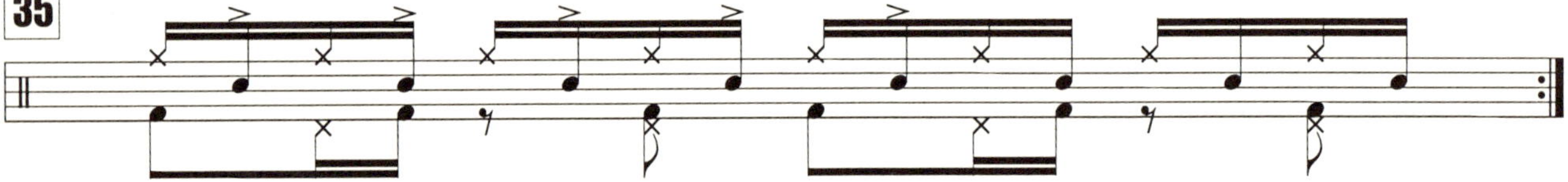

36

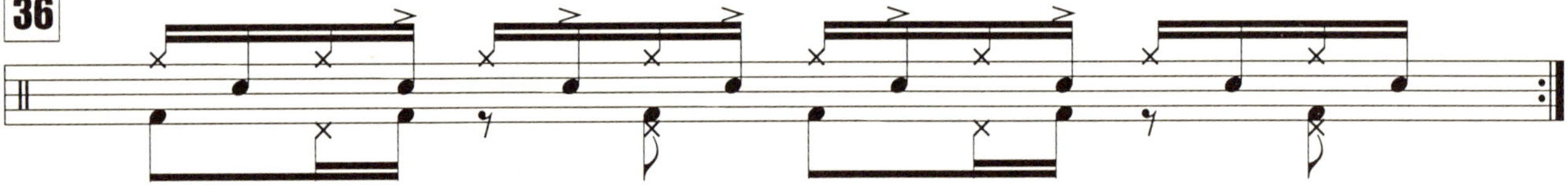

Latin Elements - Part Two

37

38

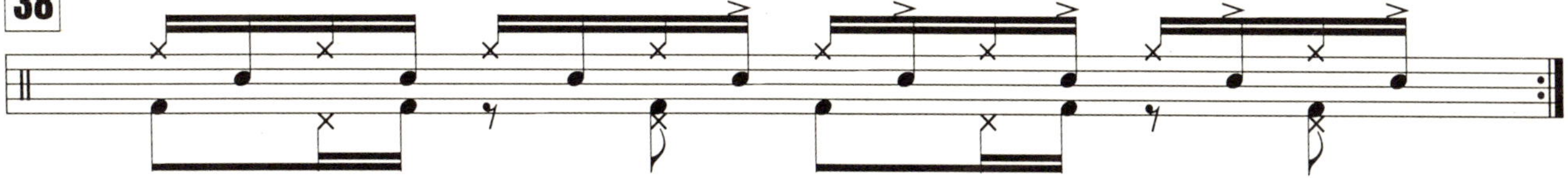

39

Latin Elements - Part Two

40

41

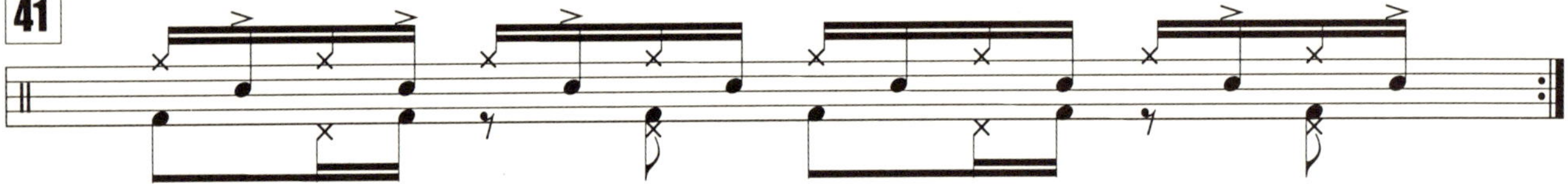

42

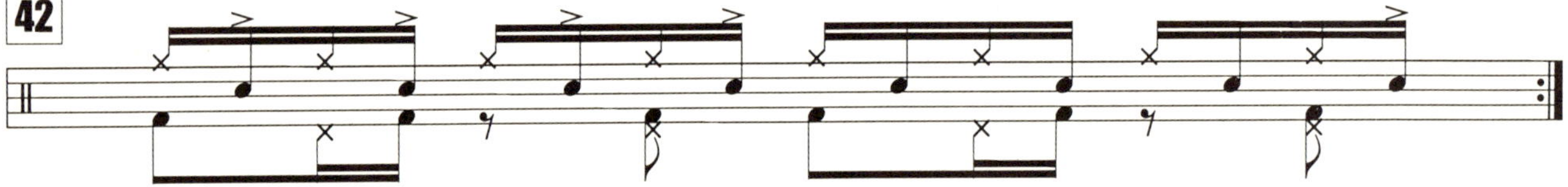

41

Latin Elements - Part Two

43

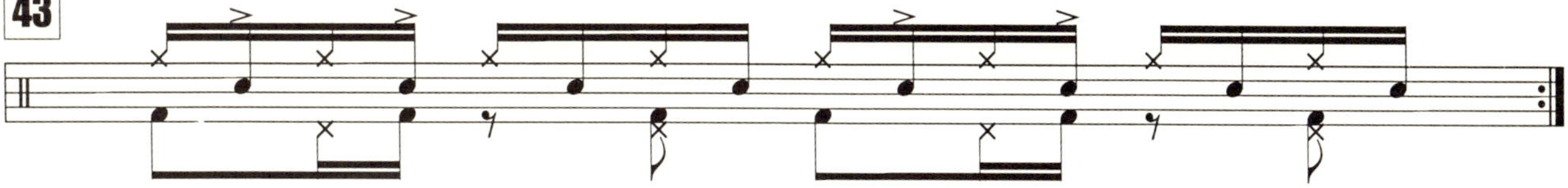

44

45

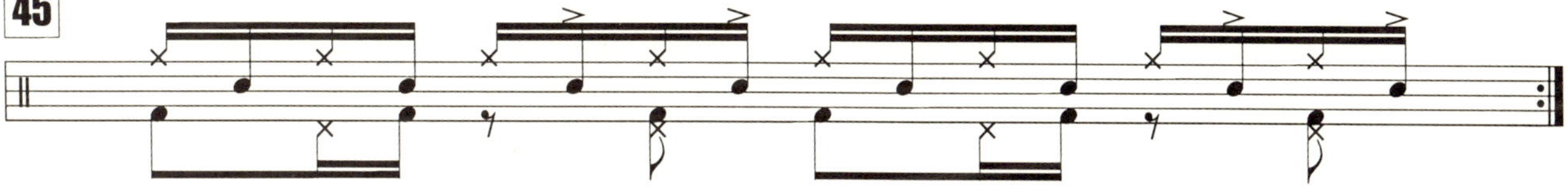

Latin Elements - Part Two

46

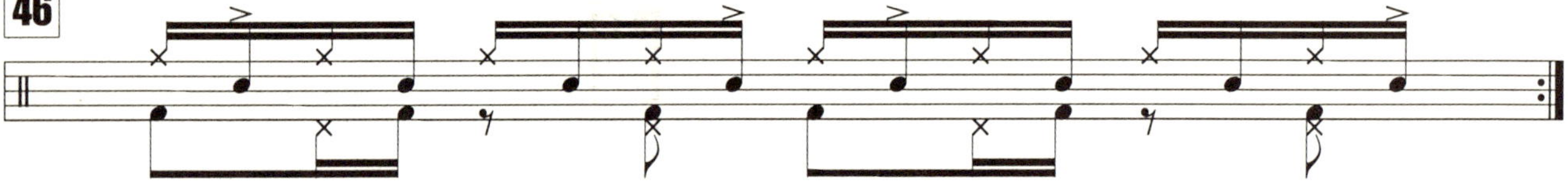

47

48

43

Latin Elements - Part Two

49

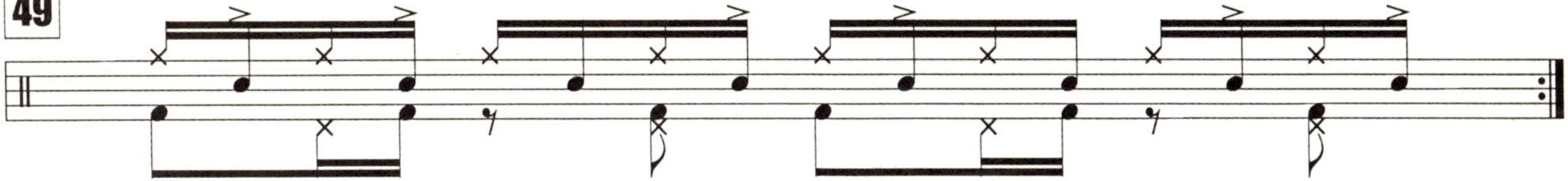

50

51

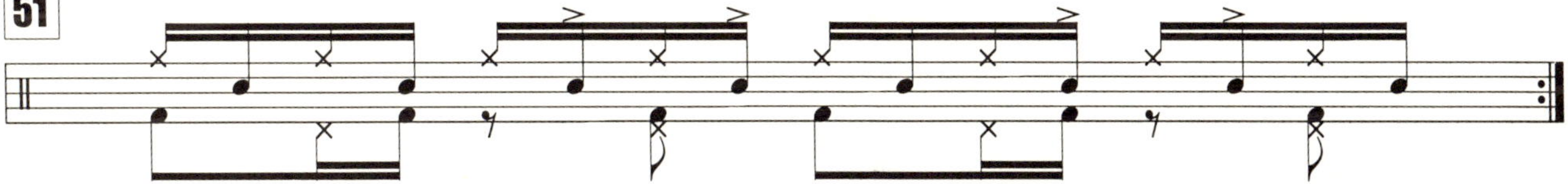

Latin Elements - Part Two

52

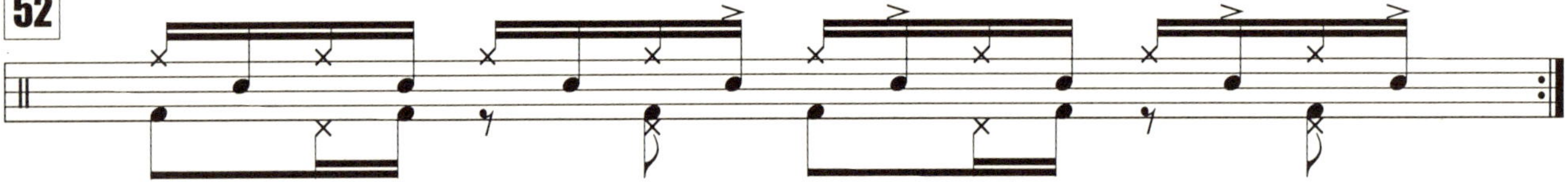

53

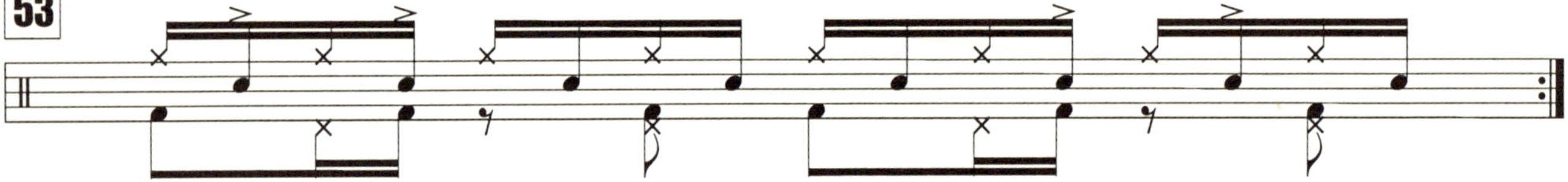

54

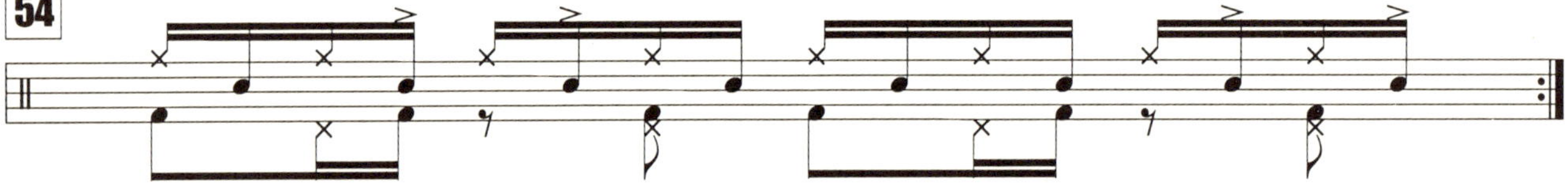

Latin Elements - Part Two

55

56

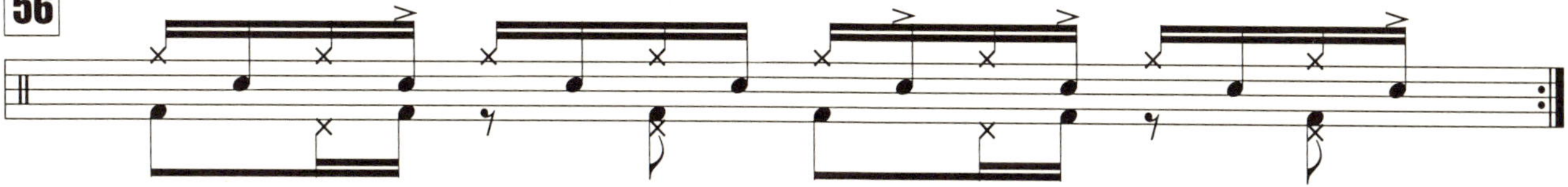

57

COMPACT disc DIGITAL AUDIO 46

Latin Elements - Part Two

58

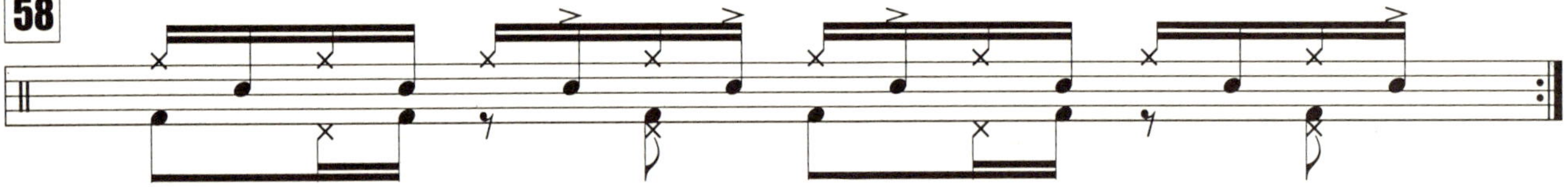

59

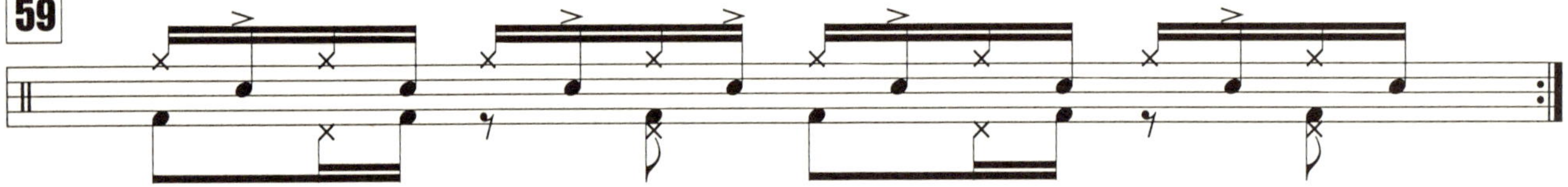

60

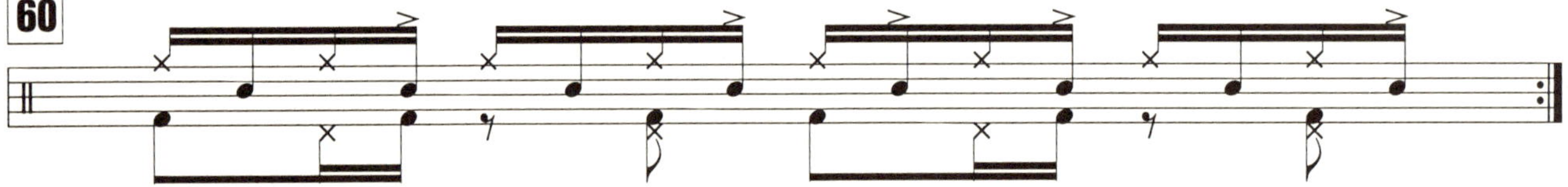

Latin Elements - Part Two

61

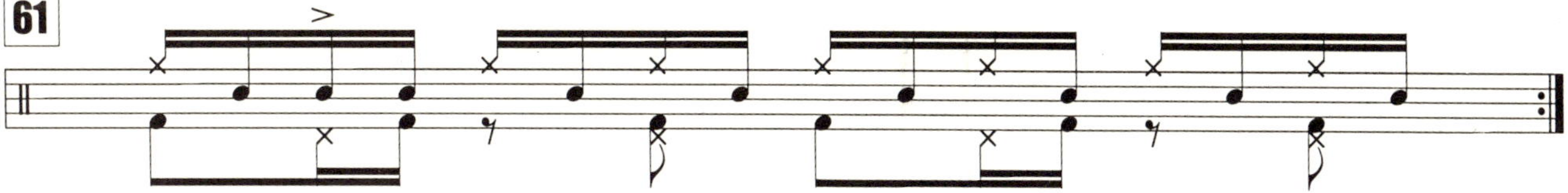

62

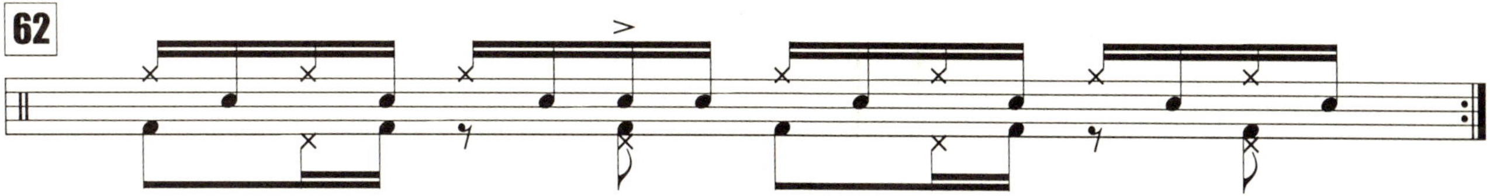

63

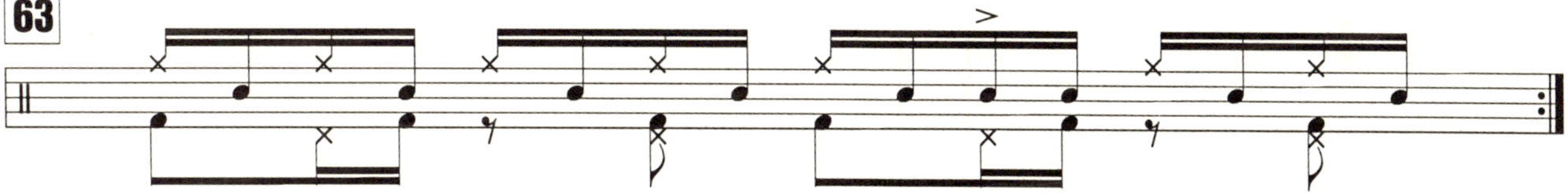

Latin Elements - Part Two

64

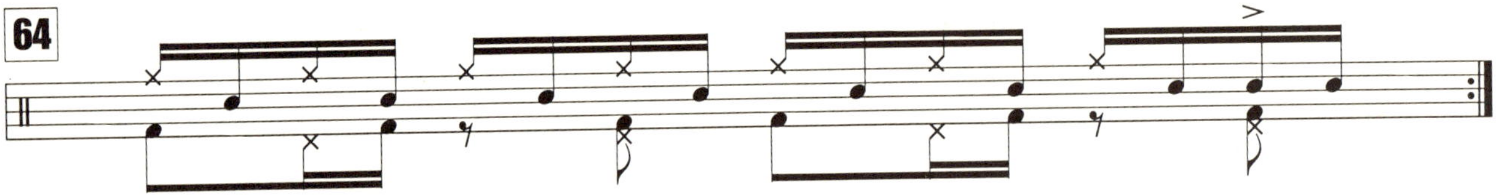

65

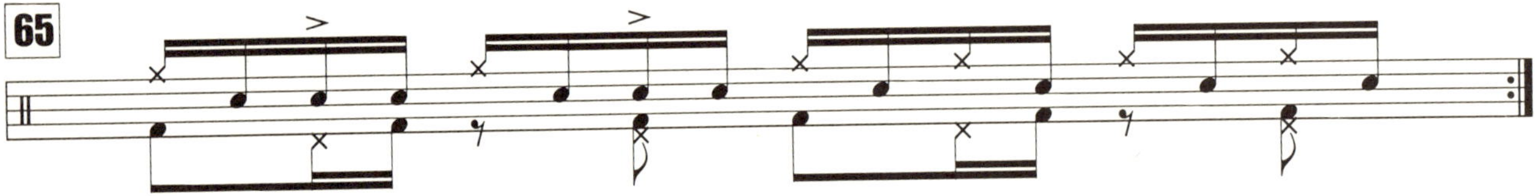

66

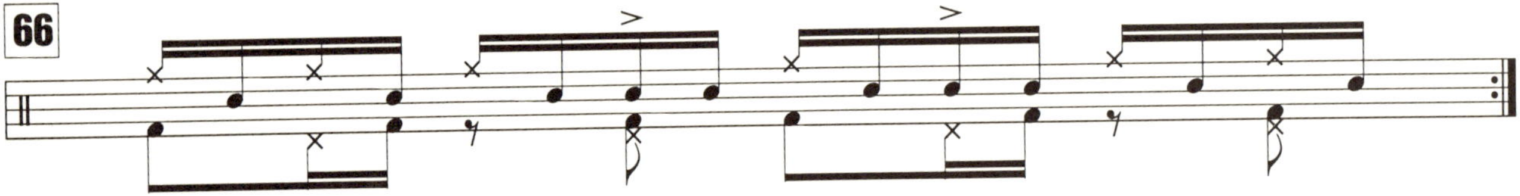

Latin Elements - Part Two

67

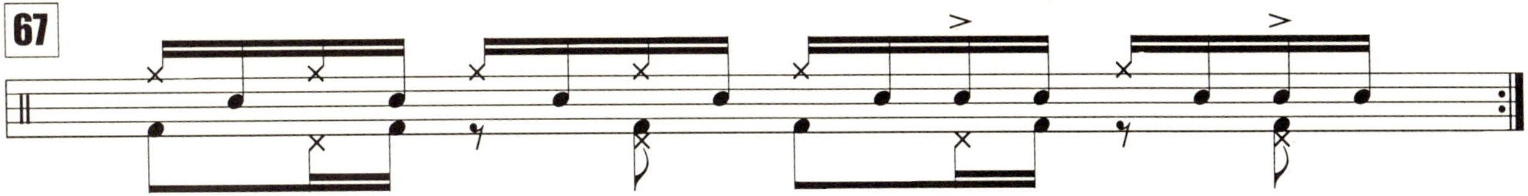

68

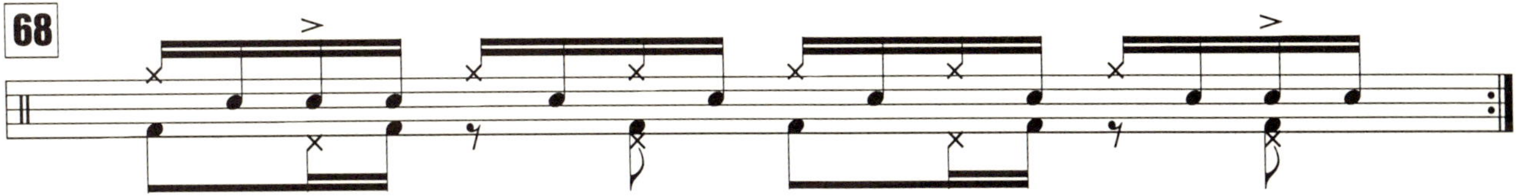

69

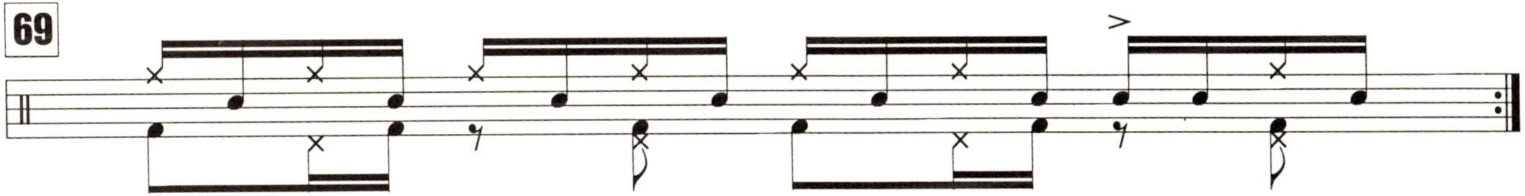

Latin Elements - Part Two

70

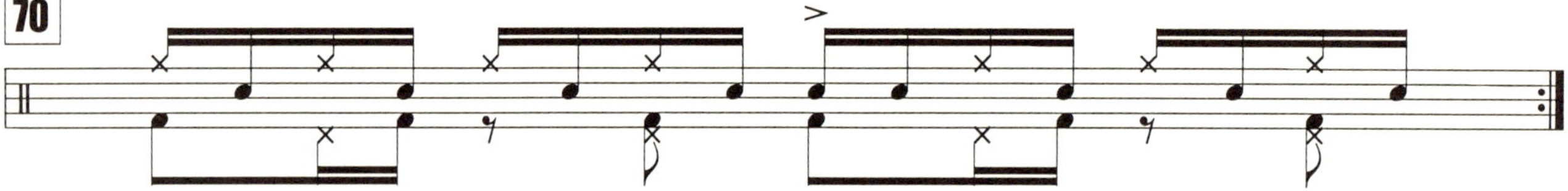

71

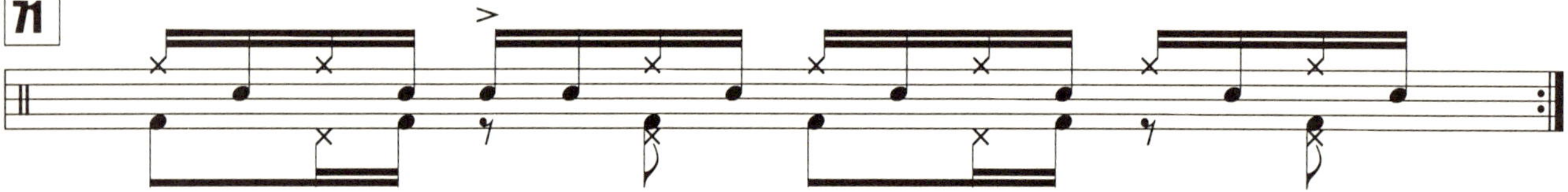

72

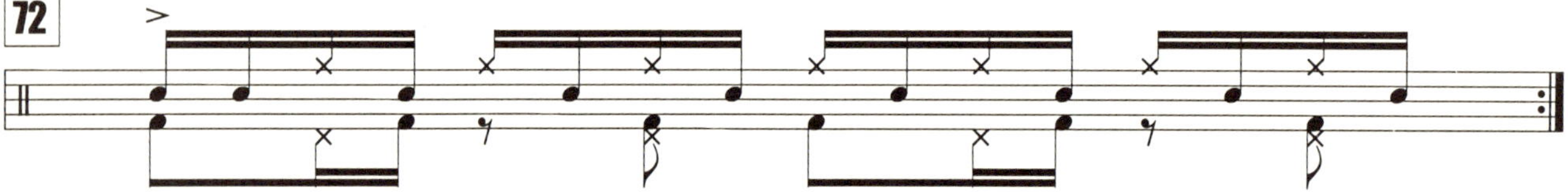

51

Latin Elements - Part Two

73

74

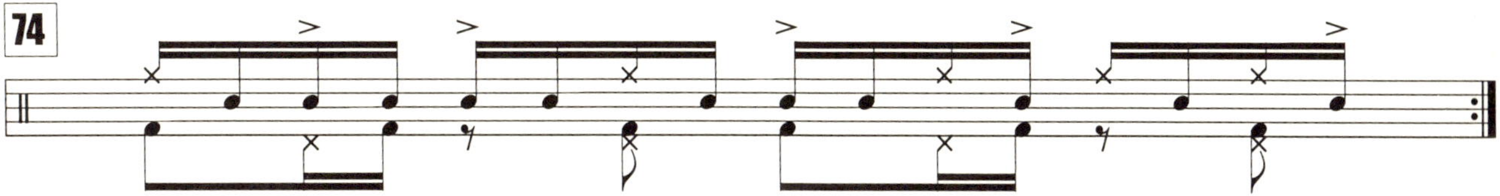

75

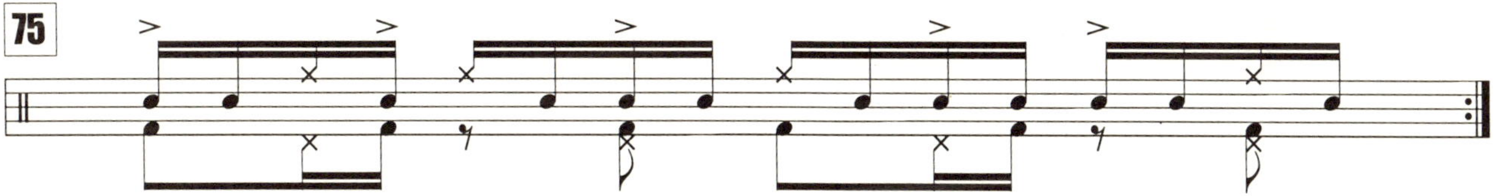

52

Latin Elements - Part Two

76

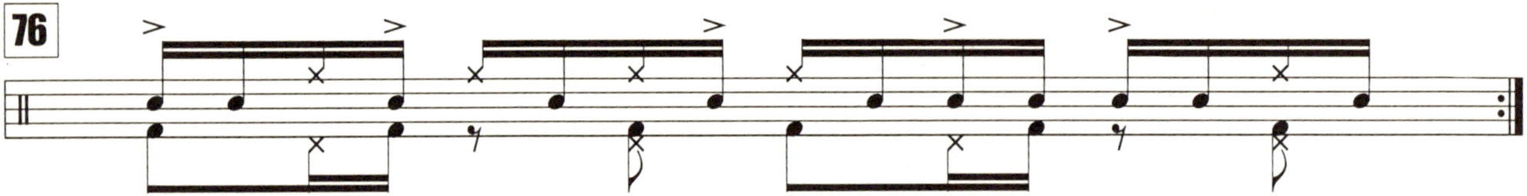

77

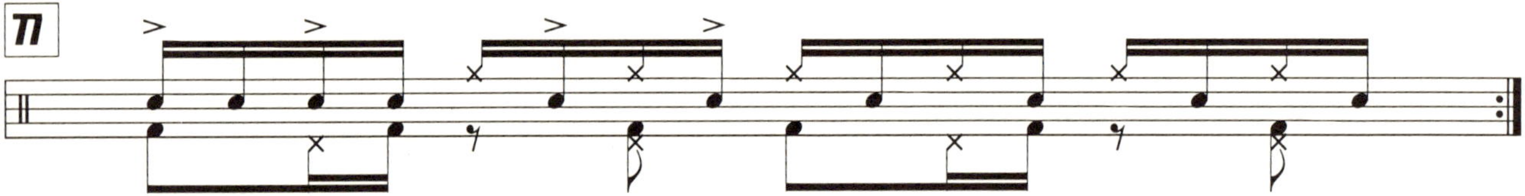

78

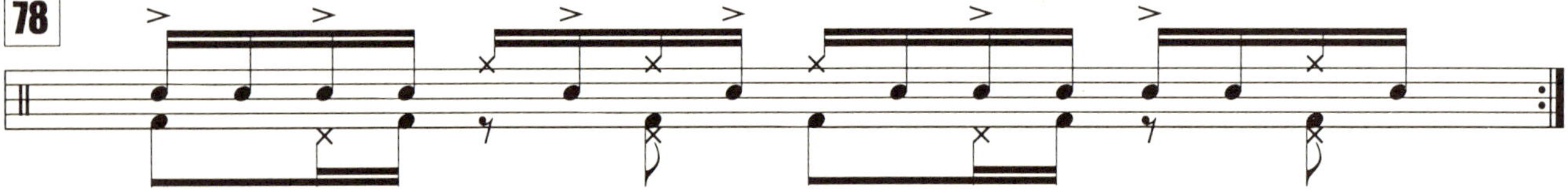

Latin Elements - Part Two

79

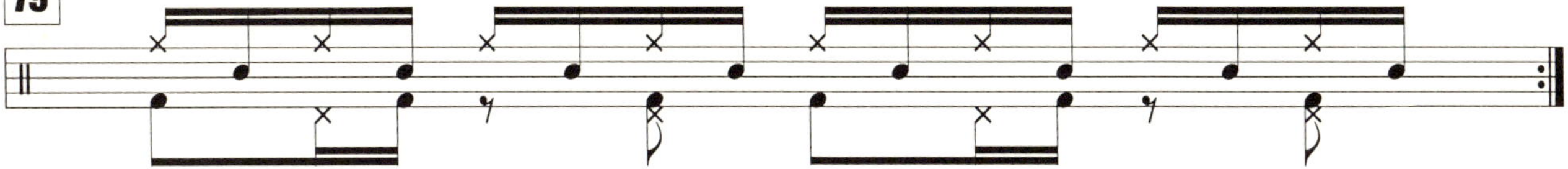

80

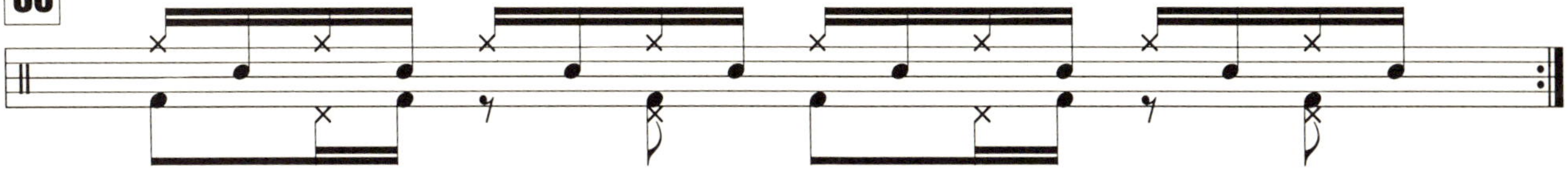

81

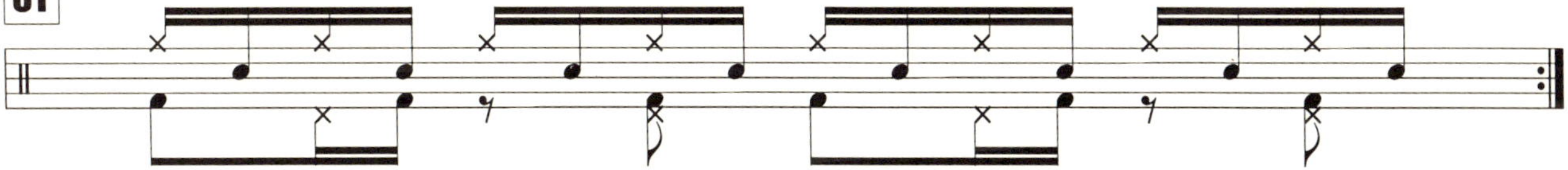

Use the following three pages as templates to write your own accents

Latin Elements - Part Two

82

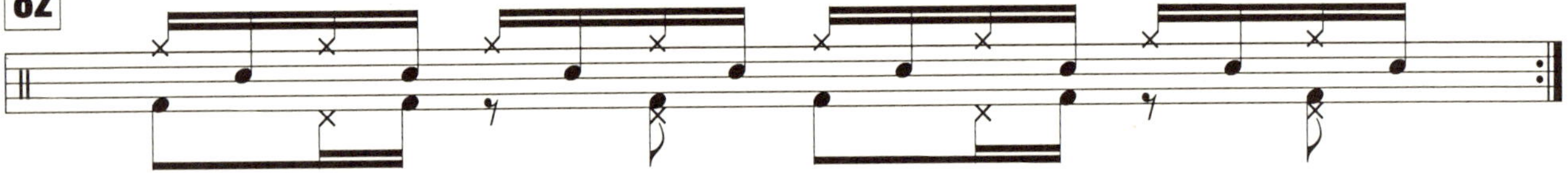

83

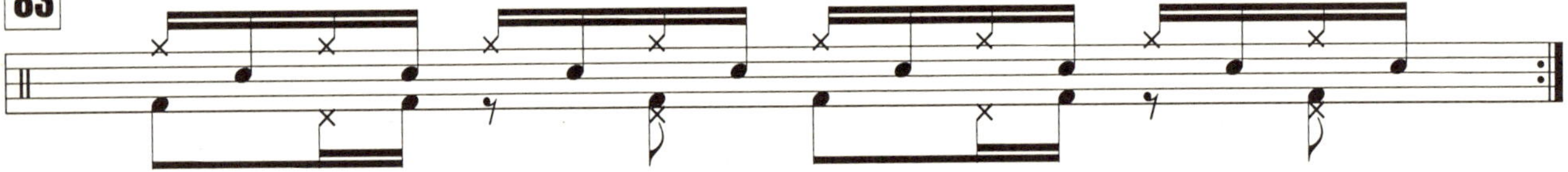

84

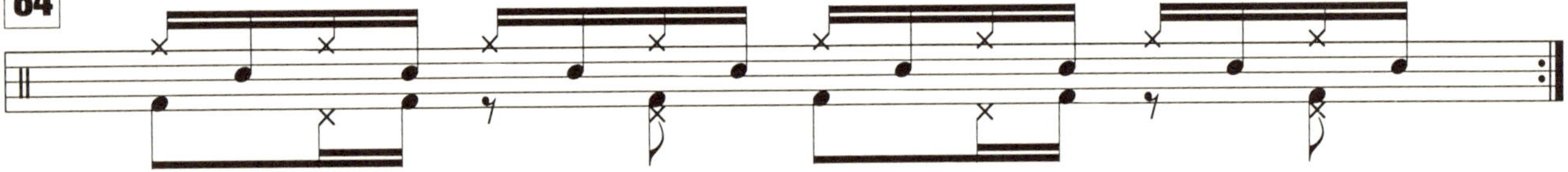

Latin Elements - Part Two

85

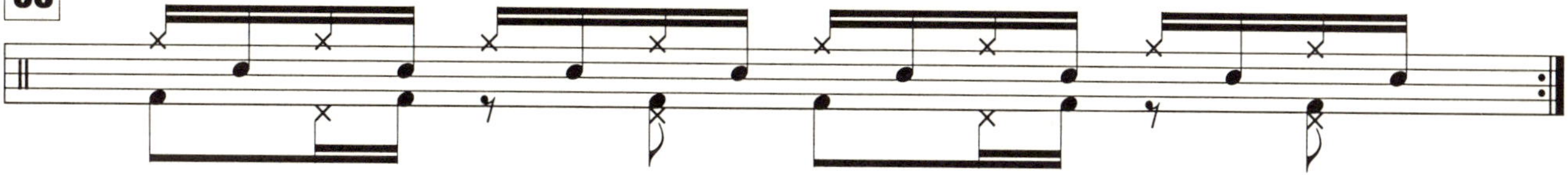

86

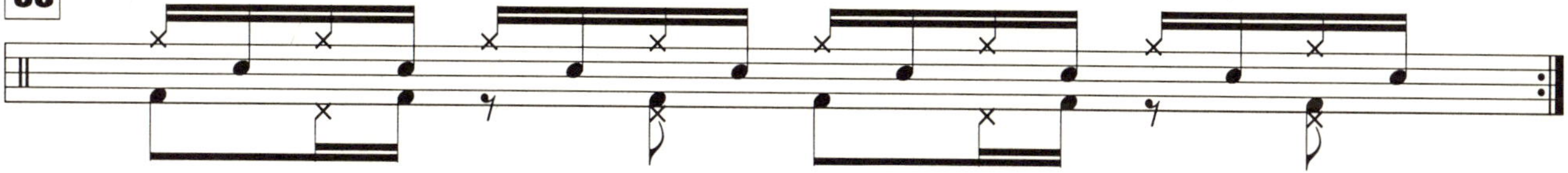

87

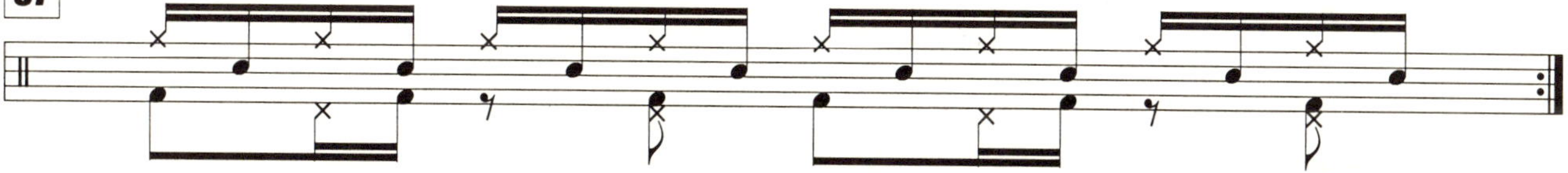